JUMP

START →

THE

SMART

VALERIE HILL

"This is a beautiful guidebook that is packed full of tips and encouragement for parents so they can enhance brain development and literacy skills for kids. The author's knowledge, dedication and love for kids shows through in this picture book, concise format for new busy parents! Pictures are a delight in the book and validate that this has been a family project! What a great gift to yourself as you begin your parenting journey, or for new parents, parents of toddlers and young school age children!"

-Mary Elijah, M.Ed.,LPC, RPT

JUMP

START

THE

SMART

Clay Bridges
PRESS

VALERIE HILL

This book is dedicated to all the new moms and dads who rise up, guiding their children and learning alongside them, step by step. You get a round of applause for opening this book!

Your baby is coming,
you're preparing the nest.
A crib, diapers, bottles, a
highchair, and all the rest!

Your family is growing,
as well as your questions,
Please allow me to share
these suggestions ...

Meet Creed, he is now 7 years old, going into first grade. Cooper is beginning high school; he is 15 years old. I've experienced the joys of raising these two boys with my husband Ryan.

Before they were born, I enjoyed the experience I had as a kindergarten teacher in our local school district. During our son's early years, I spent time as a preschool director. As I worked for many years at the accredited preschool in Houston, I realized there were certain activities and behaviors that were repeated from the infant care classroom through private preschool and pre-k classrooms. Teachers were modeling language and introducing meanings of language within dynamic sensory activities, as well as reading aloud and making print meaningful for the child early on in age-appropriate ways.

The littlest learners became increasingly confident and curiously ready to acquire letter knowledge in an environment where letters are natural and available at their eye level. The ability to acquire the skills that lead to the next stage of development was rapidly overflowing to the preschool-age rooms, advancing the skills in literacy and cognitive learning goals.

A few years after this became the standard at our preschool, I could sense why families brought their children to our school. We modeled what they did not know how to do and they did not have time to do with their child.

At my core, I'm a kindergarten teacher who loves to encourage children to be the very best they can be. Now I'd like to take some of the things I've learned from the classroom, as well as my sons' development at home and school, and share some of the best practices I've been witness to at the preschool that have produced the same qualities in other graduates too.

This book rose out of a desire to tell the story of what I have learned from my family and my work. The illustrations in the book are a mixture of both of those inspirations - some of my family and some of my school family.

I would like to be an advocate for you to have the KNOW and encourage you to make the TIME in your daily routines. Building these tips into your routines will maximize the effect and not feel as if you have more added to your workload.

Literacy, which is the ability to read and write, is the foundation to all academic studies. This idea of establishing literacy early and creating meaning with language and print has many facets. So together, we can share with you habits that set your baby up for success if you incorporate these practices early and often.

Being intentional with these habits in your routines with early learners will make the discovery come more naturally. It won't be boring schoolwork; it will flow freely out of love for your baby to support their developing brain, in whatever stage of growth they may be in.

Now, have your baby and get some rest.

You will be much better at your role of parent, enthusiast, caretaker, and now literacy advancer of your baby if you can get some sleep.

JUMP START THE SMART

TIP #1

TALK TO YOUR BABY AS IF THEY CAN UNDERSTAND YOU BECAUSE THEY DO!

Narrate what they are doing as you spend time together. They cannot always express with words, but you will see a sparkle in their eyes when you speak intently to engage. For example, when you are feeding your child say, "Let's try some peas today" or "Do you like peas?" We know they cannot respond, so we respond for them until they can. "Oh, you do like peas! Let's have another bite!"

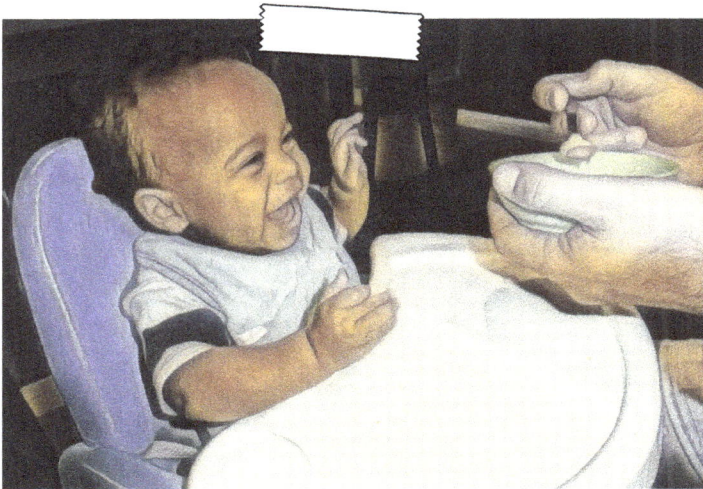

Your baby will store up the sounds of the language you supply. This will make meaning out of language as you repeat and express yourself. This type of interaction does not include any type of phone or device. It is you and your baby together, making eye contact and connection with language.

I have seen in my own children as well as the children in our school the benefit of this habit to make language and cognitive skills natural and vocabulary greater.

If they become upset when you put them down on their tummies for 3-5 minutes to build their strength to push up, get down there right next to them on your own tummy and encourage their little hearts with cheers and love.

It may be difficult to see them challenged, but again, talking them through the experience and letting them know you are there with them, soothes them with the sound of your voice and builds the muscles that need to be strengthened. This is an integral part of their brain developing to acquire and apply language when they are ready for their own talking.

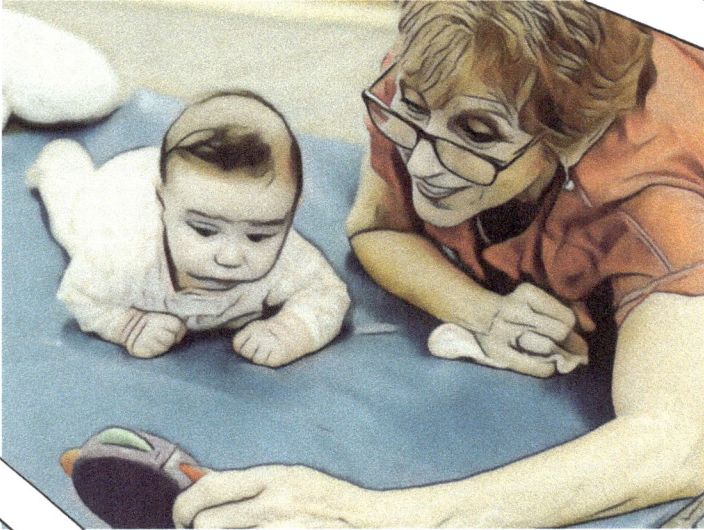

What about the moments that encourage their independence, which also allow you to have your independence for short moments? When your infant or toddler expresses their tears and discomfort when you must put them down safely to move the laundry or complete other chores, it is an opportunity to narrate what you are doing and name the emotions they are feeling as you chronicle. "Here are some blocks. You're safe here. I will go turn on the dryer and be back in a minute" or "I see your face tells me you are upset. But you are safe right now." Upon your return, reassure your child, embrace them, and say that you love and care for them.

EXPERT TIP

Happy!

MAD

SILLY

When children can name their emotions, it allows them more understanding to process and express them. At each stage of development, they can use what you have modeled continually to express in words what they may be feeling and move away from outbursts and tantrums.

TIP #2

EXPOSE YOUR CHILD TO WRITTEN WORDS AS EARLY AS INFANCY.

Read to your child each day. Indestructible board books are great in the early years. Remember to allow the child to hold the books when their motor control says they are ready. You are doing great if your child watches you with print from cookbooks, a storybook, or even an owner's manual and picks up a book to "copy" you. You'll notice them talk about the pictures to tell the story and turn the pages. Browsing the pages from left to right is another behavior they will copy from watching you.

Oh!
I see what you did there

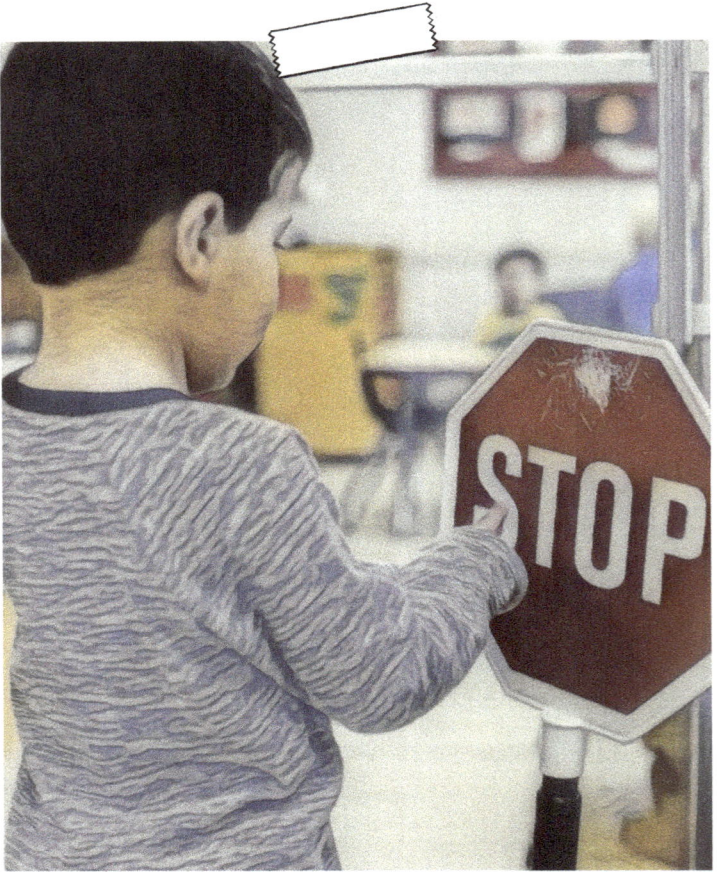

When your toddler or preschooler sees a "stop" sign or a "restroom" sign, bring it to their attention and read the words aloud as you point from left to right. You can begin to point and name letters of the alphabet to your child as opportunity allows.

Name letters as you read cereal boxes or the "goldfish" package or when your child picks out toys for their birthday wish list. You'll have a captive audience, and with that high degree of interest, they are sure to capture that letter and sound in their memory.

When you notice print on a calendar or birthday card, keep pointing to letters naming them in your day-to-day routine. A set of letters that will come up frequently is your child's name. This sequence of letters will most likely be the first letters your child will want to learn. They will see them so often, like most letters around, your child will have a natural curiosity that is attached to their sense of self.

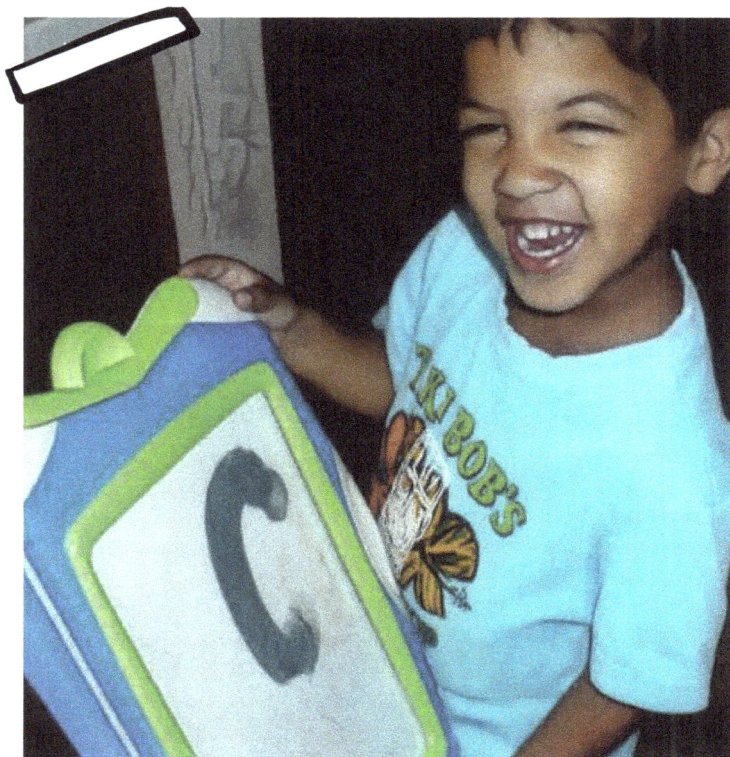

EXPERT TIP

If you want to take this to the next level of genius, find an alphabet song your child likes that has a catchy tune, or even motions associated with the sound, and play this for your child. (Dr. Jeans' Action Alphabet is a winner!) A simple letter placemat that your child can engage with is also a good tool.

Now that your child has become aware of and explored print in their environment, continue these practices. Your child is getting ready for preschool. Your child will experiment with letters and sounds through reading and writing now.

Your child is learning that letters are symbols that have meaning. As you write a grocery list, let your child write their list too. It will probably start out with scribbles at first. Accept this "list" and ask them, "Tell me what you have on your list."

If they say apples or donuts, accept their answers and dictate those words next to their 'scribbles.' The purpose of this practice is to model writing in a meaningful context for your child. They will see as you dictate a

Mom, it's not scribbling. It's my book, just like you.

grocery list or a birthday card greeting that their words are powerful and can be written. These letters have a purpose and are associated with sounds in words.

TIP #3

ALLOW THOSE LITTLE MUSCLES TO WORK!

During this stage of development, your child will benefit from many opportunities with Play-Doh, Legos, coloring, and exploring with their senses. This type of play is building their fine motor muscle control to hold a pencil or writing tool and form the shapes and symbols that will be letters soon.

To hold a pencil to write, large and fine motor muscles must be nurtured and stimulated from birth to build the connections necessary for writing and the motor coordination for movements.

This photo of Cooper creating with a bingo marker as a young toddler is an opportunity to see his small muscles strengthening to work in tandem with his eyes.

Your baby reaching and holding toys is building the foundation for this development. Large and fine motor muscles are beginning to work in coordination with one another as the child grasps a chunky toy. This is a skill necessary to hold a pencil and write later.

Not only can you see the determination on his face to achieve a sense of pride in his work, but his brain is also making connections to the language he is hearing from his caregiver about the color he is using and the shape he is painting on. The language and sounds he is hearing are being stored up to use later when he's ready to talk.

Notice the way he is grasping the marker. He is holding his helping hand up, as he is yet to develop the muscles and coordination to use it. That will come later.

TIP #4

LET THEM WRITE AND WELCOME EACH STAGE FOR IT'S GROWTH!

Take a look at some examples from each stage of writing development. It is difficult to put an age next to each one, but it's important to identify where your child may be so you can guide them to the next stage through modeling and understanding how to encourage them with letters and sounds at the right time. It would be developmentally inappropriate for a 2 year old to be writing their name from left to right, for example.

1. Random Scribbling with no control	
This stage is marked with unidentifiable scribbles	

2. Controlled Scribbles with patterns repeated	
This stage is indicative of moving the arm with greater strength and repeated movement	

3. Named Scribbles with drawings named with purpose and function	
The child understands the drawings are different from the letter like symbols created and begins to call letters names.	

4. Close Approximation with simple letters	
No order made from left to right, but the child begins to create symbolic letters. Greater control presented here begins to move towards handwriting	) ○ Ɛl ≣
5. Letter Combinations	
In this stage, children copy letters they see in long random rows with no relation to sounds. During this stage, reversals are common, yet the child believes you can read what they are expressing in their letter form.	ЯƆАН ∕∖ꟼƆ
6. Inventive Spelling	
In this stage, the child typically relates sounds with most consonants and some of the words are readable, yet unconventionally spelled. Some sight words reproduced with some punctuation. This stage can progress into sentences.	Mi MOME lovz to DK KFE!
7. Conventional Spelling	
Spelling resembles adults with correct use of vowels and capitalizations. Punctuation and proper spaces are used frequently.	My mommy loves to drink coffee. I drink my milk in the morning with her.

The child will move from scribbles to symbols and shapes all over the page. Then you will begin to see letters in random order, yet the writing begins to make meaning to the child. At this stage, they are showing that letters have a purpose. Then they begin to make sound associations with letters and pictures. This is true application of the discovery of letters and sounds when they take and use them in early reading and writings.

Name

When I grow up, I want to be....

explorer

I WOTE to be P fhSON Pn.
to PPrSPS, BeCUS Pt
outer space
IS fUNrIOUe.
yea !

"I want to be a explorer person to outer space. Because it is fun Yeah."

There will come an exciting moment when your child begins to phonetically spell and write the way they see words next to their pictures. It is not conventional spelling, but it is adorable! It's taking a risk to write the sounds the child hears and put his ideas on paper. It takes courage and tremendous effort to draw a picture and write the name next to it, such as this one from Creed's journal (shown on page 23).

As practice and fluency develop, more sentences are formed with more parts to the story. Conventional spelling will develop during elementary school years, so don't stress when you see the words spelled phonetically. It's not wrong; they are the sounds they hear in the word. That is the goal at this point. Continue to encourage the use of their sounds as they create pictures and ideas that interest them.

Along the way an understanding will be formed: My talk makes reading. Whatever I say can be written. Whatever is written can be read.

This year, Creed combined his writing skills with his play time to create a movie script. His Star Wars Legos characters were given new life with the Imperial March playing as he read his movie script aloud.

Continue to give your child lots of fun things to 'write' with even though it doesn't look like writing yet. Sidewalk chalk, crayons, and shaving cream on a bathtub wall are all fun ways to experience writing, as is spelling with letters made from pretzels or goldfish at snack time.

Playing with letters and having fun together makes the discovery of the letters occur naturally, while fine motor muscles are strengthening.

I'm Learning!

TIP #5

HELP THEM WRITE THEIR NAME.

When your child is making attempts to create symbols on paper and can identify their name in print, you can begin to introduce how to make their name. Being accepting of the work they produce during this season is important because they are making huge steps in development which involves some risk to their sense of self. Encourage them by inviting them to write as you model. They learn to write best through writing, just as they learned to talk from you talking and allowing them to mimic you. When the eyes, arms, and hands are ready to work together, your child will be ready to try their name in capital letters.

Capital letters are easier to recognize and remember than lowercase. You can demonstrate the letters in their name one letter formation at a time. They can trace the letter and then write it underneath. It is important to accept the shapes that come forth and see the progress in writing from left to right, spacing, and their pencil grip getting stronger. The correct formation of letters will come over time and with nurturing practice.

During this delicate stage of emerging as a "writer," we don't want the child to get discouraged and lose their natural desire to write. Therefore, we accept the writings they produce and model more of what we want them to imitate. As stated before, children learn to write by writing. When you support and applaud their best attempts, you will see success over time in this process.

Reading to your child every day is top priority at any stage.

Mom, you already said that

It must be important if my mom keeps saying it.

I'll say it again because sometimes people underestimate its value. Put your child in your lap and read whatever they choose for 10-15 minutes a day. As you implement this time daily, your child will acquire meaning of language in their world. They will see you modeling reading behaviors like top-to-bottom and left-to-right, holding the book correctly, self-correcting and rereading, and even taking a risk to try a new word. Besides the literacy foundations forming in these moments, the child is feeling your love for them as you

31

focus your time on them. All your attention is on them for this dedicated time. This is building up their social emotional wellbeing as they soak up the feeling of being loved. The benefits of this practice are numerous!

TIP #6

YEP, KEEP READING ALOUD

People mean well when they ask me for worksheets or extra work for them to do with their child, but the best thing you can do with your child is model what you want them to do. **Read and enjoy picture books together.**

Chants and rhythmic texts are so enjoyable for early readers and writers. Patterned texts and repeated texts should be offered to early readers such as pre k and kindergarten-age students as they have the memorization of the song to propel them into success with what they are reading. A sense of self and confidence will flow over into applying letters and sounds to reading. It seems as though they aren't really reading, and I often hear parents' comment that it's memorized. But this gives them the confidence to try the next level and become aware of how fun it really can be to learn to read.

TIP #7

WHEN YOUR CHILD IS READY, APPLY THE SOUNDS TO READ ALOUD.

Enjoying nursery rhymes and chants can help identify rhyming pairs, as well as making rhymes with word families. A word family is a base word that you then use interchangeable beginning sounds to create new words, such as man, fan, tan, can, etc. Reading a word family when you understand rhyming can establish the skills for decoding unknown words. You're showing your early reader how to apply their letter sound knowledge to blend sounds together. Blending sounds to form a word looks like this:

mmmm - aaaannnnn makes
"mmmmmaaaaaaannnnnnnn" "m-an"
"Man"

The next level is stretching out all the sounds

mmmm - aaaaaaa - nnnnnn makes
"mmmmmaaaaaaannnnnnnn" "Man"

Using letters the children can point to can be a helpful tool in blending. Our learners at this stage need tactile tools to make it real, so allowing them to move the letters they are blending together can be helpful.

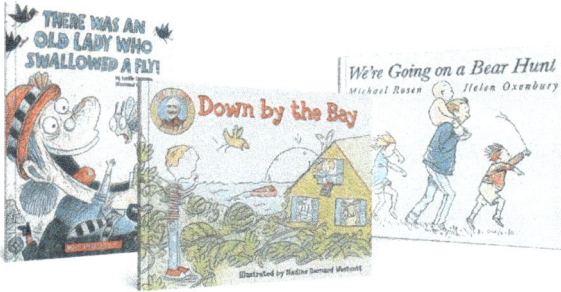

There are some books that have consistently been winners for me, but let me point out that rhyming books are especially important at this early age. Hearing the sounds that sound the same or different is a skill that is acquired through practice. Hearing the wordplay with sounds can be enjoyable for you and your young child during your time reading aloud. You'll notice some baby toys and books provide ways for you to practice making animal sounds and naming the animal associated with the sound. This skill of differentiating animal sounds is a precursor to letter-sound identification. Rhyming comes next out of this ability. Reading and rereading rhyming books children enjoy builds this skill, leading them to make rhyming pairs. This is all connected to the manipulation of sounds to decode words while reading. It's the wordplay with language.

Just keep reading aloud!

Valerie Hill

And the cliff hanger is???

Hold on,

Mom, Where is the suspense moment here???

JUMP START THE SMART

Last Tip

WHAT IF YOU WAITED TO READ THIS BOOK? WHAT IF YOUR CHILD WAS ALREADY IN PRE-K BY THE TIME YOU READ THIS BOOK? WHAT IF YOU DIDN'T KNOW? NO PROBLEM.

The human brain is a fascinating creation. It is pliable and able to make new connections all throughout your life, just the way you are learning and reading right now. Look at all the discoveries you are making today as you read through this book! So, consider this your graduation, or promotion even, to stay curious about what your child is interested in and find ways to read together and talk together. Even if you don't know the answer, let your child know "That's a great question. Let's find the answer together." Quickly phone a friend, Google it, or make the experiment happen together.

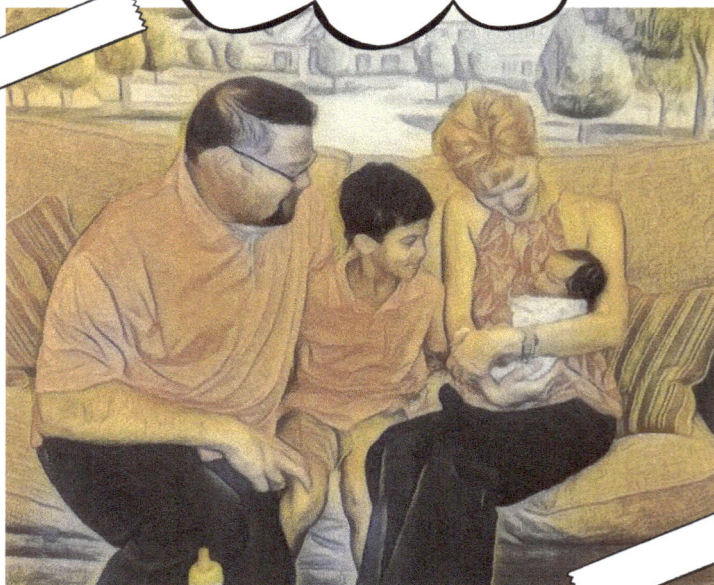

NEXT STEPS FOR A
PRESCHOOLER AT HOME:

TIPS
and →
TRICKS

Continue to show interest in what your child is doing and learning with you. You are preparing them to be a better student and reader!

⬮ When you are reading aloud, ask questions about the story. Focus on your child's comprehension of what is read. Encourage your child to predict what might come next. Point to specific letters as you read and identify rhyming words, too.

⬮ Form or trace letters on a multisensory surface. Shaving cream makes the tiles an interesting canvas for letters, and it's fun in the bathtub!

⬮ Match letters to objects around the house.

⬮ Construct letters with various household materials. Start with the letters in your child's name to add interest for your young learner.

⬮ Magnetic letters can be used early to expose your child to print. Encourage your child to explore with the letters that match letters in their name to start.

A very special thanks to all the management and teachers at Kids R Kids West Houston who are the chief learners in the classrooms, modeling for the children how to be persistent and achieve.

And to the families who have partnered with us to accomplish it!

And to all my CyLife Church family for encouraging me to share the gift God planted inside my heart for children and how we can love and teach them best.

Thank you to my husband, Ryan, for being an advocate for this project. A champion of all things clever!

I would like to recognize, with honor, Mr. Trung and Ms. Madeline Nguyen for the gift of learning they shared with me.

References:

Get Set for School by Jan Olsen, OTR and
Emily Knapton, M.Ed., OTR/L

www.ingramcontent.com/pod-product-compliance
Lightning Source LLC
Chambersburg PA
CBHW050821090426
42737CB00022B/3467